Developing Literacy

POETRY

READING AND WRITING

ACTIVITIES FOR THE LITERACY HOUR

year

3

Christine Moorcroft

Series consultant:

Ray Barker

A & C BLACK

Contents

Humour

Theme and meaning

Shape

Acknowledgments
The author and publishers are grateful to reproduce the following:
p. 12 'The Piper' by Seumus O'Sullivan reproduced with kind permission of Mrs Frances Sommerville from *Collected Poems* (Orwell Press, Dublin); p. 22 'Sea Timeless Song' reproduced with permission of Curtis Brown Ltd., London, on behalf of Grace Nichols; p. 41 'Cats' by Eleanor Farjeon from *Blackbird has spoken* published by Macmillan. Reproduced with permission of David Higham Associates Ltd., London.

Every effort has been made to trace copyright holders and to obtain their permission for use of copyright material. The author and publishers would be pleased to rectify in future editions any error or omission.

Reprinted 2002
Published 2001 by
A & C Black Publishers Limited
37 Soho Square London W1D 3QZ
www.acblack.com

ISBN O-7136-5869-X

The author and publisher would like to thank Ray Barker, Madeleine Madden, Kim Pérez and Julia Tappin for their advice in producing this series of books.

A CIP catalogue record for this book is available from the British Library.

A & C Black uses paper produced with elemental chlorine-free pulp, harvested from managed sustainable forests.

Printed in Great Britain by Caligraving Ltd, Thetford, Norfolk.

Introduction

Developing Literacy: Poetry is a series of seven photocopiable activity books for the Literacy Hour. Each book provides a range of poetry activities that support the teaching of reading and writing skills at text, sentence and word levels. They contain more than enough lesson ideas for the year for which they are intended, and provide teachers with a selection of activities to choose from.

The activities are designed to be carried out in the time allocated to independent work and incorporate strategies that encourage independent learning – for example, ways in which children can evaluate their own work or that of a partner.

The activities in **Year 3** encourage children to:

- develop their enjoyment of shape poems, poems based on observation, oral and performance poetry from different cultures and humorous poetry which plays with language;

- recite and perform poems;

- experiment with words, sounds, rhymes and rhythms;

- compose their own poems and rhymes, using some of the structures and devices of those that they read with the aid of the frameworks provided;

- use their own notes and jottings to inform their writing.

The National Literacy Strategy and poetry

The National Literacy Strategy *Framework for Teaching* encourages teachers to read all kinds of poetry and verse with children, including playground chants, nursery rhymes, action rhymes, advertisements and jingles as well as more formal poetry. The text-level objectives include teaching *about* poetry – different types of poetry, the devices used by poets, the 'messages' of poems and even the shapes of poems, plus many of the technical terms associated with poetry. Research also indicates that the ability to appreciate rhyme and rhythm has a positive effect on children's learning to read and spell.

Several word-level objectives can thus be successfully taught *through* poetry: the use of rhyme to teach about phonics and onset and rime, and of rhythm to teach about syllables.

However, teachers should not lose sight of the fun of poetry – the 'playing with words' of poets like Roger McGough and the clever use of humour by poets like Charles Causley and E V Rieu. In poetry, children can ignore the rules of grammar and put words together in new ways. And, as with other kinds of writing, the children can learn from experts. The teacher's role is to help the children to recognise a particular form of poetry, to provide a structure to help them to write it, and to help them to identify and practise the devices used by poets so that they can use them in their own poems.

Using poetry in the Literacy Hour

This book focuses on the independent part of the Literacy Hour but the notes on pages 6–8 and at the foot of each activity page suggest a variety of ways in which you can introduce poetry lessons, present whole class activities and use plenary sessions to conclude lessons. Teachers will find it useful to vary their approaches, and could also try some of the following, as appropriate for their year group:

- playing professional tape recordings of poems;

- choral speaking by individuals, small or large groups, and the whole class;

- learning poems a line or two at a time (varying the tone and expression as appropriate);

- reciting poems which have been learned;

- enacting, miming or singing poems;

- listing rhymes, alliterative or onomatopoeic words;

- clapping, tapping or stamping rhythms;

- making lists of words on a topic;

- composing poems as a group or class;

- holding small-group discussions and open forums during which the children discuss poems they have read or written.

Listening to poems

This book includes poems which need to be read to, and with, the children. Children in Year 3 can understand poems which they cannot read without help, for example extracts from works by Shakespeare. By listening to poems that they would be unable to read for themselves, the children can learn to enjoy the ideas, stories and feelings expressed in poems to which they would otherwise not have access, as well as the sounds, the rhymes and rhythms. This lays the foundations on which they can model their own poems. Listening to the poets themselves or actors reading aloud can be of special value in helping the children to enjoy a poem. At the same time, the children learn how to read poetry aloud themselves. School television programmes on poetry could be used, as could commercially available tapes: for example *Poetry Please* and *The Nation's Favourite Poems* (BBC) or *The Penguin Book of English Verse* (Penguin Classics).

At the same time, giving the children the printed work to follow will enable them to memorise some of the words, even if they cannot read them, and to recognise them when they come across them again.

Reading poems aloud

Several activities in this book ask the children to read poems aloud (both their own and those of other poets). This helps them to appreciate the poem's meaning, atmosphere and rhythm; and in the case of their own poems, to think of changes which might improve them. Sometimes, the notes that accompany an activity suggest ways in which the poems can be read aloud (for example, individuals, pairs, or groups can read the parts of different characters, or read individual lines, groups of lines, verses and choruses). The way in which a poem is spoken can make a valuable contribution to the children's understanding, appreciation and enjoyment of it, so you might experiment with different methods, depending on the poem: for example, a poem with a quiet atmosphere might be spoken using a combination of solo voices and hushed combined voices; the rhythm of a train might be created by having one group beginning to read a line while another group is finishing the previous line.

Memorising poems

Many of the activities in this book suggest that the children memorise a poem, rhyme or verse. When they memorise poetry, the children increase their vocabulary and develop the skill of using it expressively; they build up a rich store of creative ways in which words can be used, and they begin to use them themselves.

To help the children to memorise a poem, read it aloud to them, then repeat it, encouraging them to join in. Either display an enlarged copy of the poem, or work with a small group of children who each have their own copy to follow. Read a line, then cover it and ask the children to repeat it, gradually building up the number of lines covered until the children can recite the entire poem.

The following mnemonic reminds the children of how they can learn a poem:

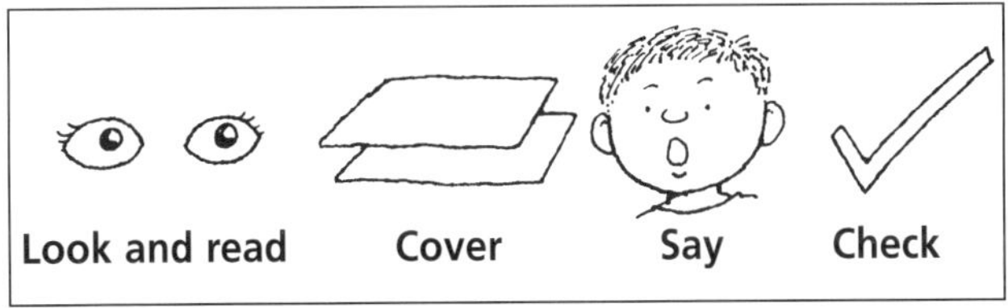

Organisation

The activities require very few resources besides scissors, glue, word-banks and simple dictionaries. Other materials are specified in the teachers' notes on the pages.

Extension activities

Most of the activity sheets end with a challenge (**Now try this!**) which reinforces and extends the children's learning and provides the teacher with an opportunity for assessment. These more challenging activities might be appropriate for only a few children; it is not expected that the whole class should complete all of them. On some pages there is space for the children to complete the extension activities, but others will require a notebook or separate sheet of paper.

The notes below expand upon those that are provided at the foot of each activity page. They give ideas and suggestions for making the most of the activity sheet, including suggestions for the whole-class introduction, the plenary session or for follow-up work using an adapted version of the activity sheet. To help teachers select appropriate learning experiences for their pupils, the activities are grouped into sections within each book, but the pages need not be presented in the order in which they appear, unless otherwise stated.

Poems for learning, reciting and performing

The poems in this section should be read aloud by the children, either taking turns during the introductory session or in groups. Give them opportunities to experiment with different ways of reading the poems aloud (including different numbers of voices for different parts of the poem), and encourage them to look out for repeated parts, such as choruses, which could be read by the whole group.

Layout (page 9) is about the effects of layout and punctuation on the reading of a poem. You could use the following as an example during the introductory session: Tilly went shopping tripping skipping jumping hopping. Alter the punctuation and layout and invite the children to read it again: for example,

> Tilly went shopping –
> Tripping, skipping,
> *Jumping*, hopping…

Peaceful poem (page 10). Five children could take turns to read a line of the poem and during the plenary session the whole class could take turns to read one of the lines they have written. It could be practised for performance during assembly.

After reading **Sound effects** (page 11) and carrying out the activities, the children could paint pictures of a scene conjured up by the poem. Their pictures could be displayed alongside copies of their descriptions of sound effects. Useful materials for sound effects include: percussion instruments, straw, twigs, bubble-wrapping, tea-towels or similar pieces of material, pan lids, cans, sticks, boxes, combs and tissue paper.

Poetry in action: 1 and 2 (pages 12–13). Focus on the way in which punctuation helps you to read the poem. Some lines run straight into the next one without a pause: ask the children to identify those lines as well as the pauses. Ask them also to notice the effect of the repetition of 'away' in line 3, the repetition of 'and' at the beginnings of lines 6, 7 and 8 and the way in which rhyme contributes to the rhythm. The children should notice that the poem begins with a quiet street in which a piper takes out his pipe and then plays one or two notes before launching into the tune which draws everyone out into the street until the street is full of people dancing to the rhythm of an Irish jig. At the end the piper stops playing and it is as if all the people suddenly go back to their ordinary everyday activities: the street is quiet once more.

Market poem (page 14) provides the beginning of, and a framework for writing, a poem which the children complete and then perform. Encourage them first to make notes of anything which might be sold at a market and then to look for rhyming pairs of words  and to add descriptions which fit the rhythm.

The effects of words

The activities in this section develop the children's appreciation of the ways in which poets use words to create effects.

Native American names (page 15) encourages the children to think of adjectives which convey an impression of an object. They could try different adjectives with the same noun and compare the effects.

Hot or cold, wet or dry: 1 and 2 (pages 16–17). On blank spinners the children could write words with other meanings: for example, old, new, dull and bright. There should be nine words for each meaning.

Spooky poem (page 18) concentrates on the effects of words. It could be linked with sentence-level work on adjectives and verbs. A source of spooky poems suitable for this age group is *Young Hippo Spooky Poems* compiled by Jennifer Curry (Scholastic, 1998); classic poems which are also suitable include 'The Ghosts' High Noon' (W S Gilbert), 'The Witches' Chant' (from Shakespeare's *Macbeth*), 'The Ghoul' (Jack Prelutsky) and 'The Visitor' (Ian Serraillier).

Adjective poems (page 19) could be continued long after the children have completed this activity: they could write and display adjective poems for others to guess the subjects. Class readings could be organised in which a child reads his or her poem a line at a time while the others see how soon they can work out what is being described.

A waterfall of verbs (page 20) presents an extract from *'The Cataract of Lodore'*, by Robert Southey, a poem which must contain more verbs than most others in the English language! If possible read the poem in its entirety (it is in *The Oxford Book of Children's Verse*) – the children could use it as a word-bank on water.

Words with feelings (page 21) focuses on the 'feel' created by the sounds of words. There are no hard-and-fast answers, and some words can belong in more than one set. The following answers are suggested: (gentle) a smile of light, downy flake, leafy glen, soft-scratching, (powerful) charging, cracking ice, crying wind, mighty monster, roaring and wild, turmoil seething, volleyed and thundered, waves roaring, winds howling; (fast) charging, flashing past, hurtles by, swifter and swifter, whistle by; (slow) downy flake, lazily lifting, motionless moon, no stir in the air.

Rhythm

The activities in this section help the children to recognise different types of rhythms and to develop their appreciation of the effects of these rhythms. The children are encouraged to explore the rhythms they hear in everyday life.

On and on (page 22) provides an example of a poem in which words are repeated to create an effect (the rhythm of the sea). One group of children could repeat quietly 'sea timeless' while another group (simultaneously) reads the entire poem, with the whole class joining in the last four lines of each verse.

Day and night (page 23) provides another example of a poem in which words are repeated to create an effect (of the day waking up). Compare its lively opening with that of *'The Piper'* (page 12). It presents the day as if it were human: this lays a foundation for later work on personification.

Rhyme

These activities encourage the children to explore rhyme for its own sake and to enjoy the sounds of words. They also develop the children's appreciation of different rhyme patterns.

Travel rhymes (page 24). Possible answers include: swim to Lymm, ski to Dundee, sail to Hale, flee to Dundee, speed to the Tweed, row to Stowe, ride to Hyde, skate to Margate and crawl to Porthcawl. Possible answers for the extension activity are: walk to York (or Cork or Dundalk), dance to France, fly to Skye (or Rye) and tear to Ware. The children could also look for places which rhyme with scamper, skid, trot, roll, hop, skip, run, jig, race, skate, leap, wade, paddle, and so on.

Monday's child (page 25) gives the children a model on which to base a simple rhyming poem. The rhyme-finder provides pairs of rhyming words from which the children can choose; encourage them to think up others of their own.

Rhyme pattern (page 26) has rhyming words in the same lines as well as at the ends of lines: for example, honey and money and owl and fowl. The children should follow the same rhyme pattern in the extension activity.

What is a breeze? (page 27) encourages the children to make up poetry which does not rhyme. Discuss the format of the example questions (' What is …?') and the ways in which they are answered (the answers are what someone imagines, rather than scientific explanations). The children could compare them with the kinds of answers they try to find for scientific questions.

Poetic description and devices

These activities explore the initial sounds of words and encourage the children to notice the effect of the repetition of these sounds in poems.

Heavy or light, Catch the hatchet! and **Onomatopoeia collections** (pages 28–30) draw attention to the effects of words. The children could also list words which sound rough or smooth, soft or hard. Useful words for page 29 include batch, crotchet, crutch, ditch, each, fetch, hatch, hotch-potch, ketchup, latch, match, patch, ratchet, scratch, stitch, touch and watch.

Alliterative allsorts (page 31) focuses on the main consonant sounds in words. The children could look for alliteration in poems they read. Possible answers are: a bunch of bananas, a bottle of beer, a hunk of ham, a dish of damsons, a chunk of cheese, a cup of cocoa, a lump of lard, a basket of bread, a mug of milk, a slice of sausage, a bowl of berries, a litre of liquid, a pan of pasta, a plate of potatoes, a tank of terrapins and a can of carrots.

Still as a post and tall as a spire and **Comparisons** (pages 32–33) can be linked with work on similes. The children could make collections of comparisons or similes they come across in their reading.

Humour

Here the children are encouraged to enjoy nonsense poems and poems which explore words and ideas, and to play tricks with tongue-twisters and riddles.

Ptarmigans and pterodactyls (page 34) invites the children to explore the sounds of words with silent letters and to make up new ones. It develops their ability to recognise, and create their own humour with word-play.

Word jokes (page 35). Examples with which to introduce the activity include words whose letters are exchanged and others whose opening sounds are exchanged but with different spellings: for example jelly beans/belly jeans, skipping rope/ripping scope. This activity could be linked with work on onset and rime. *Answers*: mad bunny, cat-flap, cold ghost, making toast.

Absurd words (page 36). Other words with more than one meaning which the children could explore include eye, foot, head. They could make up jokes about the words: for example, a needle gives sharp looks with its eye. *Answers*: the bonnet of a car, a car boot, a disc jockey, a daffodil bulb, fingernails, the tongue of a shoe, the mouth of a tunnel, the wings of a building, a cricket bat and a fish finger.

Legs riddle (page 37) is an old riddle about a man or woman who sits on a three-legged stool with a leg of lamb (or other meat) in a bag; a dog or cat runs off with the meat, the man or woman jumps up and throws the stool after the animal and makes it bring back the meat. Some children might need help: for example, 'think of things with three legs/two legs…' and so on.

Twister (page 38) gives an extract from an old tongue-twister which is difficult to read slowly, let alone quickly. Discuss the phonemes which cause the difficulty (the sequence of 's' and 'th' sounds). The children might need to be reminded of the different ways of spelling the 's' phoneme: 's', 'ss', 'ce'.

A parrot's advice and **A parent's advice** (pages 39–40) present a model upon which the children can base their own poems featuring advice from a mother or father to a child. Encourage them to imagine a 'dream' reward for the child.

Theme and meaning

This section develops the children's skills in classifying poems by theme or subject, and invites them to compare poems on the same theme and by the same poet.

The same but different: 1 and 2 (pages 41–42) provide two poems about the same subject. The children should notice that the first poet seems to like cats and presents them as taking very little notice of people – doing just as they like, in fact ('They don't care!'). The second poet presents the cat as hating people and as evil (with words such as 'the hate of a million years', 'snaky tail' and 'demon's tail'). For a class anthology the children could also cut out cat shapes on which to write poems they come across about cats.

Wind words: 1 and 2 (pages 43–44) help the children to collect notes which could be used in presenting different views of the same subject (the wind): a strong, destructive wind and a gentle breeze. They could think of other rough, hostile-sounding words to describe the first picture and gentle, friendly-sounding words to describe the second.

Shape

These pages introduce shape poems and invite the children to explore the effects of layout on a poem and the ways in which the shape can be an integral part of the poem.

Splash poem, **Shape sentences** and **Word shapes** (pages 45–47) explore poems and poetic sentences whose shape reflects their subject and provides frameworks for the children to use. Examples (from *The Works*, published by Macmillan) include '*AND IT'S A…*' (Rita Ray), '*The Shape I'm in*' (James Carter), and '*Rhythm Machine*' (Trevor Harvey) .

In **Calligrams** (page 48) the words themselves are formed in shapes which express something about the subject-matter. It provides ideas to help the children to use their imagination to create their own calligrams.

Layout

- **Read aloud 1a, then 2a.**
- **Make notes about the differences.**
- **Do the same with 1b and 2b, and 1c and 2c.**

1a. Wild winds call call. Rain hail fall fall. Fresh gales squall squall. Tossed trees tall tall. Crash down all all.

1b. Up the airy mountain down the rushy glen. We daren't go a-hunting for fear of little men.

1c. Is the moon tired? She looks so pale within her misty veil; she scales the sky from east to west and takes no rest.

2a. Wild winds call, call.

Rain, hail fall, fall.

Fresh gales squall, squall.

Tossed trees tall, tall.

Crash down all, all.

2b. Up the airy mountain,
Down the rushy glen,
We daren't go a-hunting,
For fear of little men.

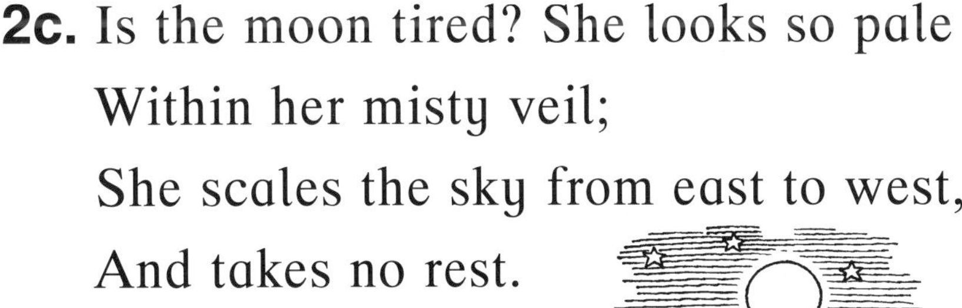

2c. Is the moon tired? She looks so pale
Within her misty veil;
She scales the sky from east to west,
And takes no rest.

- **Which way do you think the poets wrote them? How can you tell?**

Teachers' note During the introductory session discuss the effects of punctuation and layout on the reader: write a sentence on the board (see Introduction page 6), and invite the children to take turns to read it aloud; then alter the punctuation and layout of the sentence and ask them to re-read it. What is the difference?

Developing Literacy
Poetry Year 3
© A & C Black

Peaceful poem

Celtic Benediction

Deep peace of the Running Wave to you.
Deep peace of the Flowing Air to you.
Deep peace of the Quiet Earth to you.
Deep peace of the Shining Stars to you.
Deep peace of the Son of Peace to you.

Anonymous

• With your group, read the poem aloud in different ways. Which sounds the best?

1. One voice ☐

Two voices together ☐

The whole group together ☐

2. The same voices reading every line ☐

Two voices taking turns to read a line ☐

One voice reading a line and then the whole group reading a line ☐

• Write your own 'Celtic Benediction'.

Teachers' note Do the children know that a benediction is a blessing? They should notice the peaceful atmosphere of the poem; in the extension activity they could write the first four lines of a new verse for the poem, retaining the last line, which is the main part of the benediction.

**Developing Literacy
Poetry Year 3
© A & C Black**

Sound effects

- **Read the poem.**
- **Now try out different ways of making the sounds.**
- **Write the best ones in the boxes.**

Wind Song

When the wind blows
The quiet things speak.
Some whisper, some clang;
Some creak.

Grasses swish.
Treetops sigh.
Flags slap
and snap at the sky.
Wires on poles
whistle and hum.
Ashcans roll.
Windows drum.

When the wind goes –
suddenly
then,
the quiet things
are quiet again.

Lillian Moore

tissue paper or leaves run through fingers

- **Work in a group. Make the sound effects as you read the poem aloud.**

Teachers' note Discuss the changes of sound in the poem: it begins very quietly ('The quiet things speak'), sounds are heard, one by one, and then suddenly they stop. Ask the children why the sounds stop. Have available materials with which the children can experiment to produce sound effects to represent the sounds described in the poem (they could also use their voices).

Developing Literacy
Poetry Year 3
© A & C Black

Poetry in action: 1

A Piper

A piper in the streets today
Set up, and tuned, and started to play,
And away, away, away on the tide
Of his music we started; on every side
Doors and windows were opened wide,
And men left down their work and came,
And women with petticoats coloured like flame.
And little bare feet that were blue with cold,
Went dancing back to the age of gold,
And all the world went gay, went gay,
For half an hour in the street today.

Seumus O'Sullivan

- **Number the lines in the poem 1 to 11.**
- **Imagine the street. In the boxes,
  write what you can see and hear.**

Just before the poem begins

In lines 1 and 2

Teachers' note Read the poem aloud. It begins hesitantly, with a few notes of the pipe (note the commas); the rhythm of a jig develops in the third line and ends on the last line (when the people stop dancing and return to their work). Ask the children to imagine the poem as a series of scenes in a play or film. What would they see and hear? Continued on page 13.

**Developing Literacy
Poetry Year 3
© A & C Black**

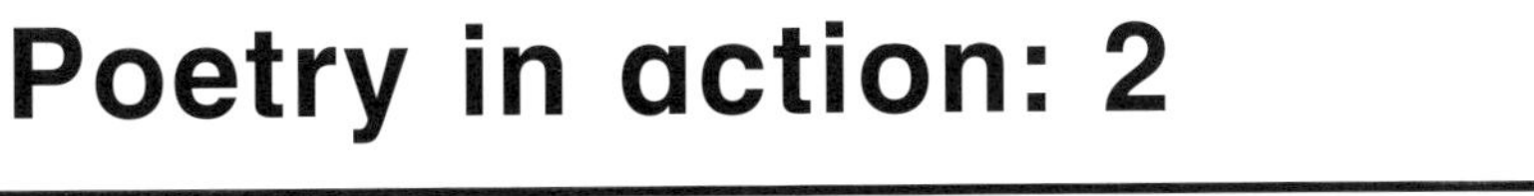

Poetry in action: 2

In lines 3 to 5

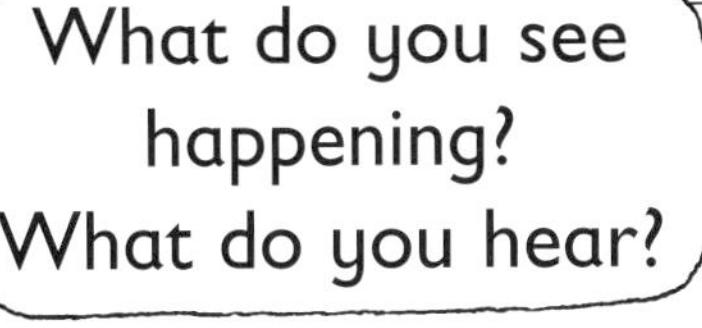

In line 6

In line 7

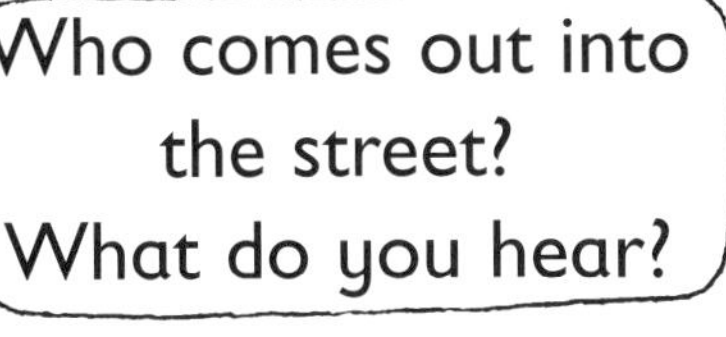

In line 8

In lines 9 to 11

After the end of the poem

Teachers' note The children should begin this activity on page 12. As an extension activity, some children might be able to write stage directions for enacting the poem while it is read aloud.

**Developing Literacy
Poetry Year 3
© A & C Black**

Market poem

What else might the market traders call?

- **Write on the notepad.**

knives and forks
bottles and corks

freshly-baked ham
strawberry jam

- **Write three verses for the market poem.**

- **Perform the poem with your group.**

Teachers' note Read the verse to the children and ask them for suggestions on how it could be performed by a group: how many people should read each line (the same person or different ones?) and how many should read the chorus? Invite a group to demonstrate their ideas.

**Developing Literacy
Poetry Year 3
© A & C Black**

Native American names

Native American people often have
names that describe things in nature.

From the water-fall he named her,
Minnehaha, Laughing Water...
from *Hiawatha* by Henry Wadsworth Longfellow

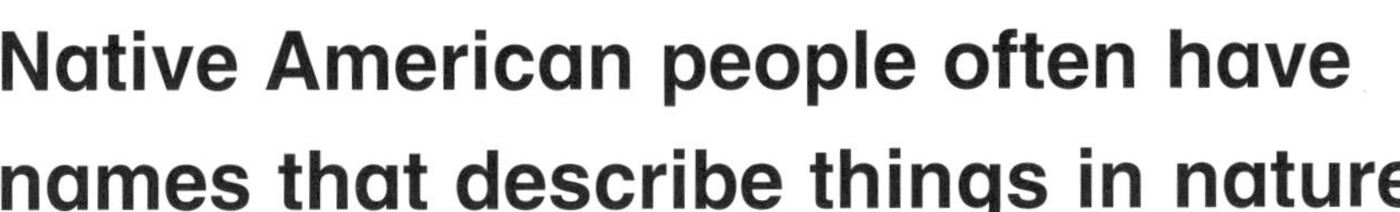

- **Write adjectives to make your
  own names from nature.**

 _Mighty_ Eagle

 _________ Cloud

 _________ Rock

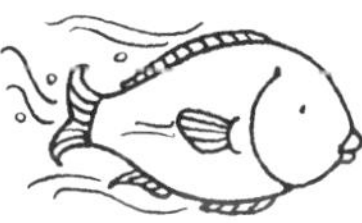 _________ Fish

 _________ Snowflake

 _________ Butterfly

 _________ Mountain

 _________ Leaf

 _________ Star

 _________ Wolf

 _________ Sun

 _________ Grass

 _________ Moon

 _________ Rain

- **Make up names from nature for yourself,
  your family and your friends.**

Teachers' note Introduce the activity by naming things in nature other than those mentioned
on this page and ask the children to supply adjectives: for example, moth, ladybird, thunder,
lightning. The child who supplies the adjective has a turn to name something in nature and the
others try to think of an adjective, and so on.

**Developing Literacy
Poetry Year 3**
© A & C Black

Hot or cold, wet or dry: 1

Choose one of these meanings:

hot , cold , wet **or** dry .

- **Take turns to spin the spinner. If you spin a word which has your meaning, write it on the chart. The first player to collect nine words wins.**

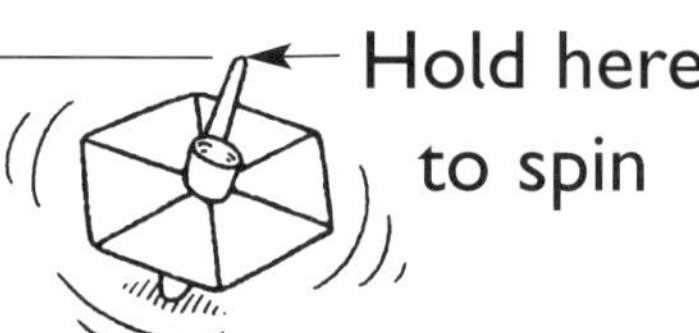

hot	cold	wet	dry

- **Use the words from the chart to write about a place you know.**

Teachers' note Copy page 17 on to card. The children cut out the spinners and push the cap of a ball-point pen through the centre of each spinner (a short pencil or a cocktail stick can be used, but ball-point pen tops work the best – hold the pocket clip to spin). Continued on page 17.

Developing Literacy
Poetry Year 3
© A & C Black

Hot or cold, wet or dry: 2

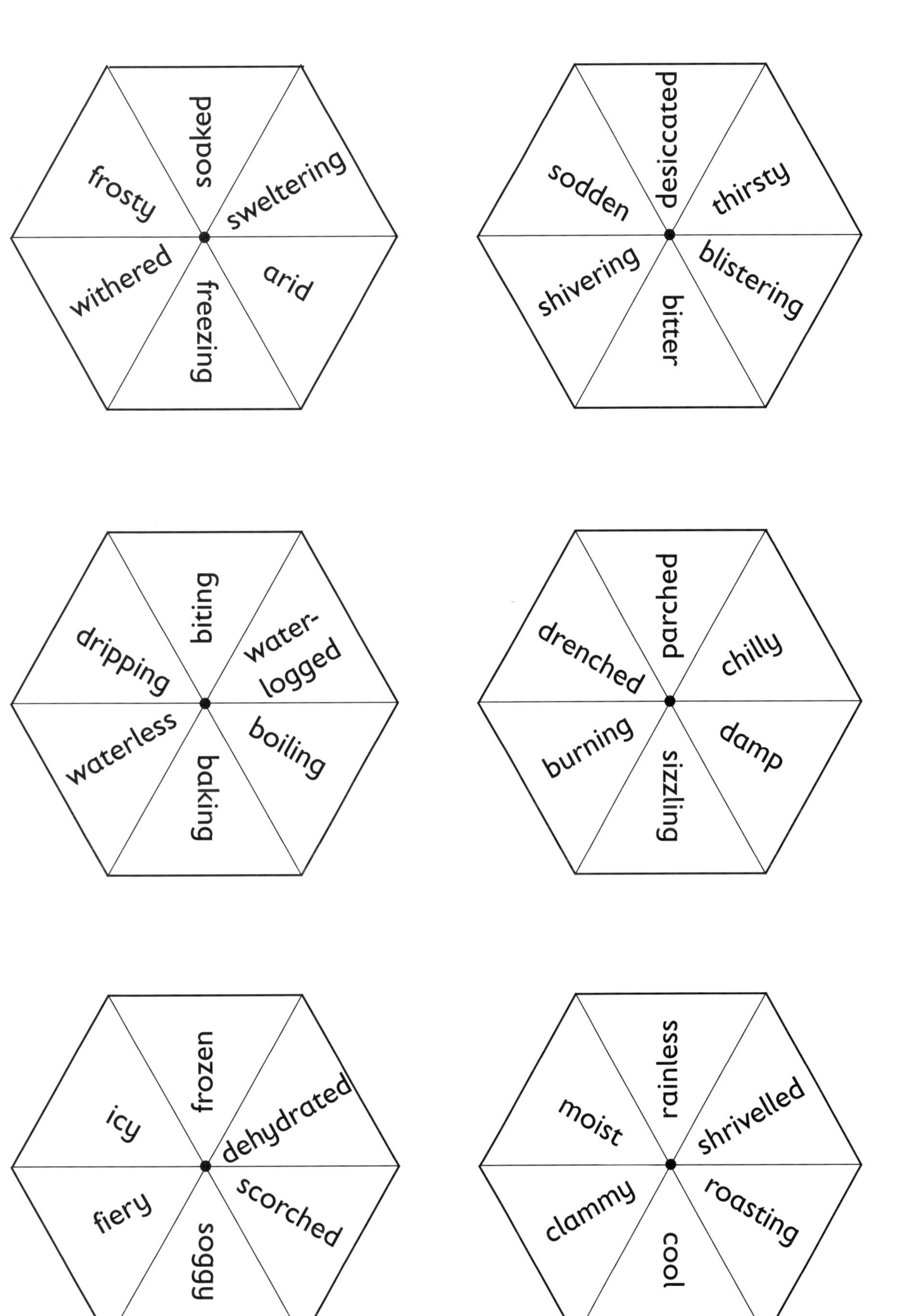

Developing Literacy
Poetry Year 3
© A & C Black

Spooky poem

- **Write adjectives and verbs which make the old house seem spooky.**

Adjectives

creaky

Verbs

rattle

- **Arrange the adjectives and verbs to make a spooky poem.**

____

____

____

____

____

____

Teachers' note Before the children begin this activity they should have had the opportunity to read 'spooky' poems (see **Introduction** page 6). Ask them to suggest 'spooky' words to describe the old house and to suggest 'spooky' things which might happen there.

Developing Literacy
Poetry Year 3
© A & C Black

Adjective poems

Simon wrote an `adjective poem` **about the sky like this.**

Notes	Using a thesaurus	The finished poem
blue	azure	Azure,
high	cloudless	Cloudless.
clear	sunny	Immense,
big	vast	Never-ending.
bright	immense	Near,
huge	never-ending	Far,
far	distant	High –
near		The sky.

• **Write an adjective poem about a tree you have seen.**

Notes	Using a	The finished poem
		____________
		____________
		____________
		____________
		____________
		____________
		____________

• **Write an adjective poem about something else. Miss out the last line.**

• **Give the poem to a partner. Can they guess what you are describing?**

Teachers' note Discuss the way in which Simon began working on his poem, the way in which he used a thesaurus to increase the number of words from which he could choose, how he decided which words to use, the order in which to write them and how to punctuate his poem, and how he finally names the subject at the end.

**Developing Literacy
Poetry Year 3
© A & C Black**

A waterfall of verbs

- **Underline the verbs in this poem.**
- **What do they tell you about the water?**

____

____

____

____

____

- **Write two sets of verbs that tell you about the actions of the wind.**

Use a dictionary.

Rising and leaping,
Sinking and creeping,
Swelling and sweeping,
Showering and springing,
Flying and flinging,
Writhing and ringing,
Eddying and whisking,
Spouting and frisking,
Turning and twisting,
Around and around
With endless rebound!
Smiting and fighting,
A sight to delight in;
Confounding, astounding,
Dizzying and deafening the ear with its sound.

From *The Cataract of Lodore* by Robert Southey

- **Use a set of verbs in a poem about the Sun.**

Teachers' note If possible, read the poem in its entirety (see **Introduction** page 7) and ask the children to notice the verbs which the poet uses for the movement of water. What kind of picture does the poem create? They could think of other verbs for much slower-moving water, write a poem and compare the picture it conjures up with that of the poem on this page.

Developing Literacy
Poetry Year 3
© A & C Black

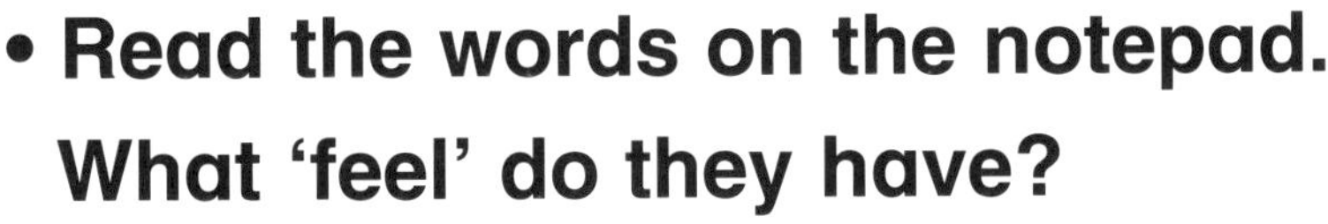

Words with feelings

- **Read the words on the notepad.**
  What 'feel' do they have?
- **Write them where you think they belong.**

Use a dictionary.

Some words might belong in more than one box.

Gentle

a smile of light

Powerful

Fast

Slow

a smile of light
charging
cracking ice
crying wind
downy flake
flashing past
hurtles by
leafy glen
lazily lifting
mighty monster
motionless moon
no stir in the air
roaring and wild
soft-scratching
swifter and swifter
turmoil seething
volleyed and thundered
waves roaring
whistle by
winds howling

Now try this!

- **Find other words in poems to add to the boxes.**

Teachers' note Tell the children that the words in the notepad come from poems. Invite them to take turns to read aloud a word from the notepad. Encourage the children to look up words they do not know.

**Developing Literacy
Poetry Year 3
© A & C Black**

On and on

- **Read the poem.**
- **Underline the** repeated words **.**
- **What goes on forever?**

  ____

- **Which three things change?**

  ____

  ____

  ____

- **List other things which might change, or come and go.**

Sea Timeless Song

Hurricane come
and hurricane go
but sea – sea timeless
sea timeless
sea timeless
sea timeless
sea timeless

Hibiscus bloom
then dry-wither so
but sea – sea timeless
sea timeless
sea timeless
sea timeless
sea timeless

Tourist come
and tourist go
but sea – sea timeless
sea timeless
sea timeless
sea timeless
sea timeless

Grace Nichols

- **Write another verse for the poem.**

  ____

  ____

  ____

  ____

  ____

Teachers' note Ask the children what they notice about the rhythm of the repeated lines and why the poet has repeated them. They should notice that they have the rhythm of waves washing in and out on the shore. Discuss the things in the poem which change and the things which do not. The children could go on to make up a class 'Sea Timeless Song'.

Developing Literacy
Poetry Year 3
© A & C Black

Day and night

- **What is the poem about?**

  ____

  How could you change it to a poem about nightfall?
- **Underline the words you would change.**
- **On the notepad write words you could use instead.**

The World is Day-Breaking

The world is day-breaking!
The world is day-breaking!

Day arises
From its sleep.
Day wakes up
With the dawning light.
The world is day-breaking!
The world is day-breaking!

Anonymous

- **Use your notes to help you write a poem about nightfall.**

  The world is _______________________

  ____

  ____

  ____

  ____

  ____

  ____

Teachers' note Ask the children what they notice about the pattern of the poem. They should notice the repeated lines and their effect – of a gradual awakening, rather like someone opening his or her eyes, yawning and stretching.

**Developing Literacy
Poetry Year 3
© A & C Black**

Travel rhymes

- **Read the first rhyme.**
- **Fill in the gaps with verbs
  that rhyme with the places.**

- **Write place names to rhyme with the verbs.**

- **Write four others.**

Teachers' note Read the first two examples with the children and ask them to suggest rhyming verbs for the next two or three. The verbs should all be in some way linked with travelling. For the extension activity provide atlases, including United Kingdom road atlases which list even the smallest villages.

Developing Literacy
Poetry Year 3
© A & C Black

24

Monday's child

• **Read the poem.**

Monday's child is fair of face,
Tuesday's child is full of grace,
Wednesday's child is full of woe,
Thursday's child has far to go,
Friday's child is loving and giving,
Saturday's child works hard for a living,
But the child who is born on the Sabbath day
Is bonny and blithe and good and gay.

Anonymous

• **Use the rhyme-finder to help you write other words**
for the poem.

Rhyme-finder

dear	deed	care
fear	need	share
live	heart	kind
give	part	mind
sadness	brothers	healthy
gladness	others	wealthy

caring
daring

Monday's child is *always healthy*

Tuesday's child is _______________________

Wednesday's child is _______________________

____

____

____

____

**Developing Literacy
Poetry Year 3
© A & C Black**

Rhyme pattern

- **Underline the rhymes in the poem.**
- **Number the lines. Start each verse with `1`.**

- **Which lines rhyme?**

____

____

- **Find other places where there are rhymes. Give examples.**

____

____

The Owl and the Pussy-Cat

The Owl and the Pussy-Cat went to sea
　　In a beautiful pea-green boat:
They took some honey, and plenty of money
　　Wrapped up in a five-pound note.
The Owl looked up to the stars above,
　　And sang to a small guitar,
'O lovely Pussy, O Pussy, my love,
　What a beautiful Pussy you are,
　　　　You are,
　　　　You are!
What a beautiful Pussy you are!'

Pussy said to the Owl, 'You elegant fowl,
　　How charmingly sweet you sing!
Oh! Let us be married; too long we have tarried:
　　But what shall we do for a ring?'
They sailed away for a year and a day,
　　To the land where the Bong-tree grows;
And there in a wood a Piggy-wig stood,
　　With a ring at the end of his nose,
　　　　His nose,
　　　　His nose,
With a ring at the end of his nose.

Edward Lear

- **Change the word `boat` to `ship`, and `honey` to `jam`.**
- **Which rhyming words need to change?**
- **Re-write the verse with the new rhymes.**

Teachers' note Before the children begin the activity read the poem aloud so that they can enjoy the story, the words and the sounds before they look for the rhymes in it. Point out that rhymes are not only at the ends of the lines and ask the children to point out any they can find in the first verse which are not at the ends of the lines.

**Developing Literacy
Poetry Year 3
© A & C Black**

What is a breeze?

Poems do not have to rhyme.

- **Complete this** question and answer poem.
Make up your own answers.

What is a breeze?
The breath of an angel.
When do butterflies sleep?
When flowers sing to them.
What is a cloud?

____

Why is the sky blue?

____

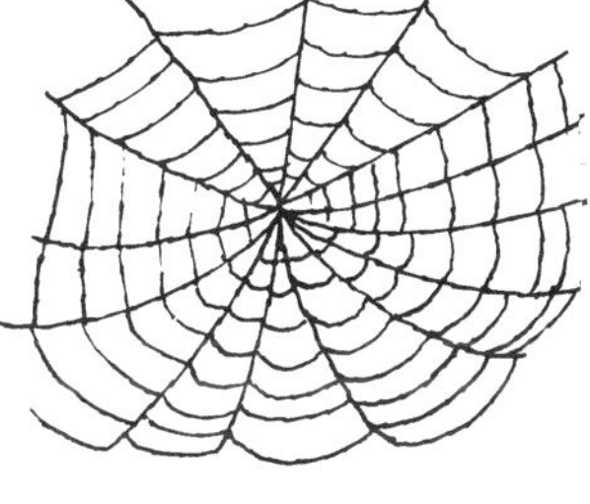

What makes bees buzz?

____

What are cobwebs made of?

____

What makes owls smile?

____

What makes mice cry?

____

- **Make up five other questions like the ones in the poem. Give them to a partner to answer.**

Teachers' note Encourage the children to think of imaginative definitions by giving examples, such as: 'What is the Sun?' – 'The central heating of the universe', 'What is rain?' – 'The tears of the clouds' and 'Why do stars twinkle?' – 'Because they are the jewels of the sky.'

**Developing Literacy
Poetry Year 3
© A & C Black**

Heavy or light

- **Say the words in the box. Listen to their sounds.**
- **Write the words in the correct bags.**

air	dread	knob	peep
barge	fall	leap	ping
blip	flab	lump	plod
clang	glee	may	rubble
clod	hip	mud	sail
dip	ice	mug	waddle

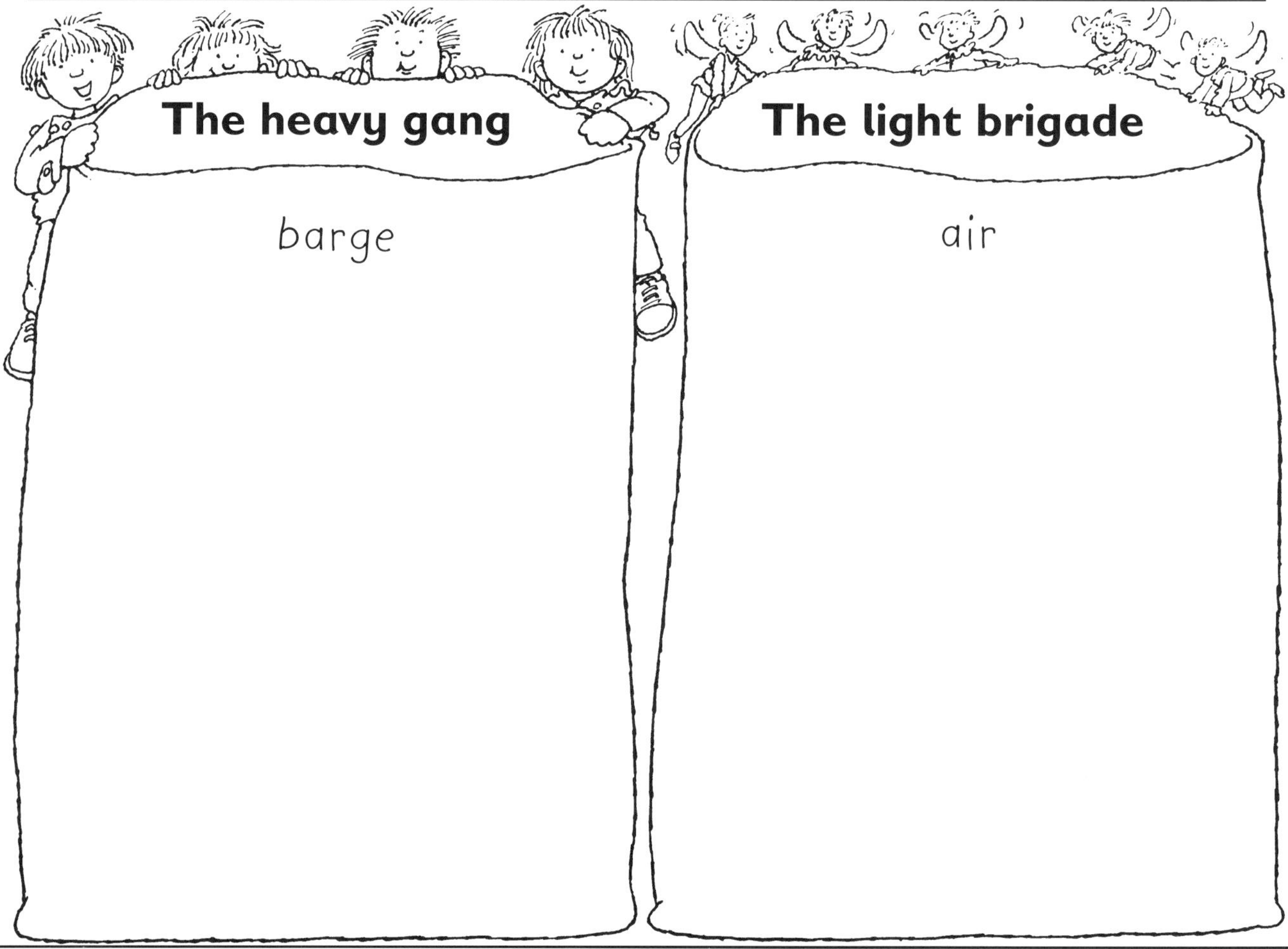

The heavy gang

barge

The light brigade

air

- **Write four more words in each bag.**
- **Write four lines for a heavy or light poem.**

Teachers' note With the children, read some of the words in the box aloud and ask them to listen to the sound of each word and to say 'heavy' or 'light' after each one. Other heavy-sounding words include clomp, clump, flog, slog and slump; other light-sounding words include fairy, sing, sip, sky and tip.

Developing Literacy
Poetry Year 3
© A & C Black

Catch the hatchet!

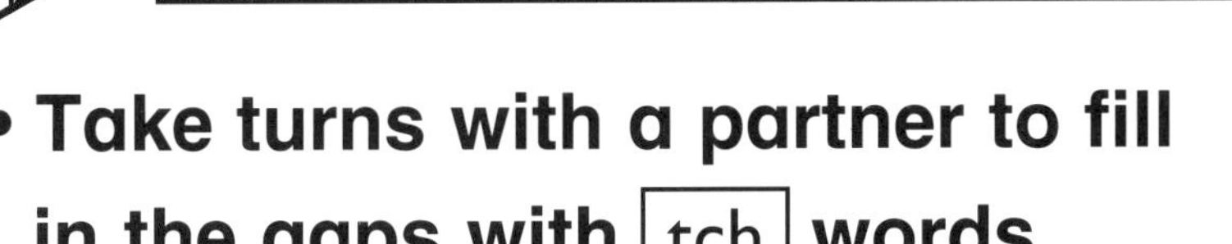

- **Take turns with a partner to fill in the gaps with** `tch` **words.**

- **Read the poem you have made. Does it sound fast or slow?** _______

- **List some words which have a smooth sound. Use some of them to write a poem with a slow movement.**

Teachers' note Discuss the quick, jerky effect of a series of 'tch' words. The children could first try this activity orally, taking turns to add a 'tch' word (the words should have the 'tch' sound, but their spellings need not include the letter string: for example, rich, such and much).

Developing Literacy
Poetry Year 3
© A & C Black

Onomatopoeia collections

Words which have onomatopoeia **really sound like their meanings.**

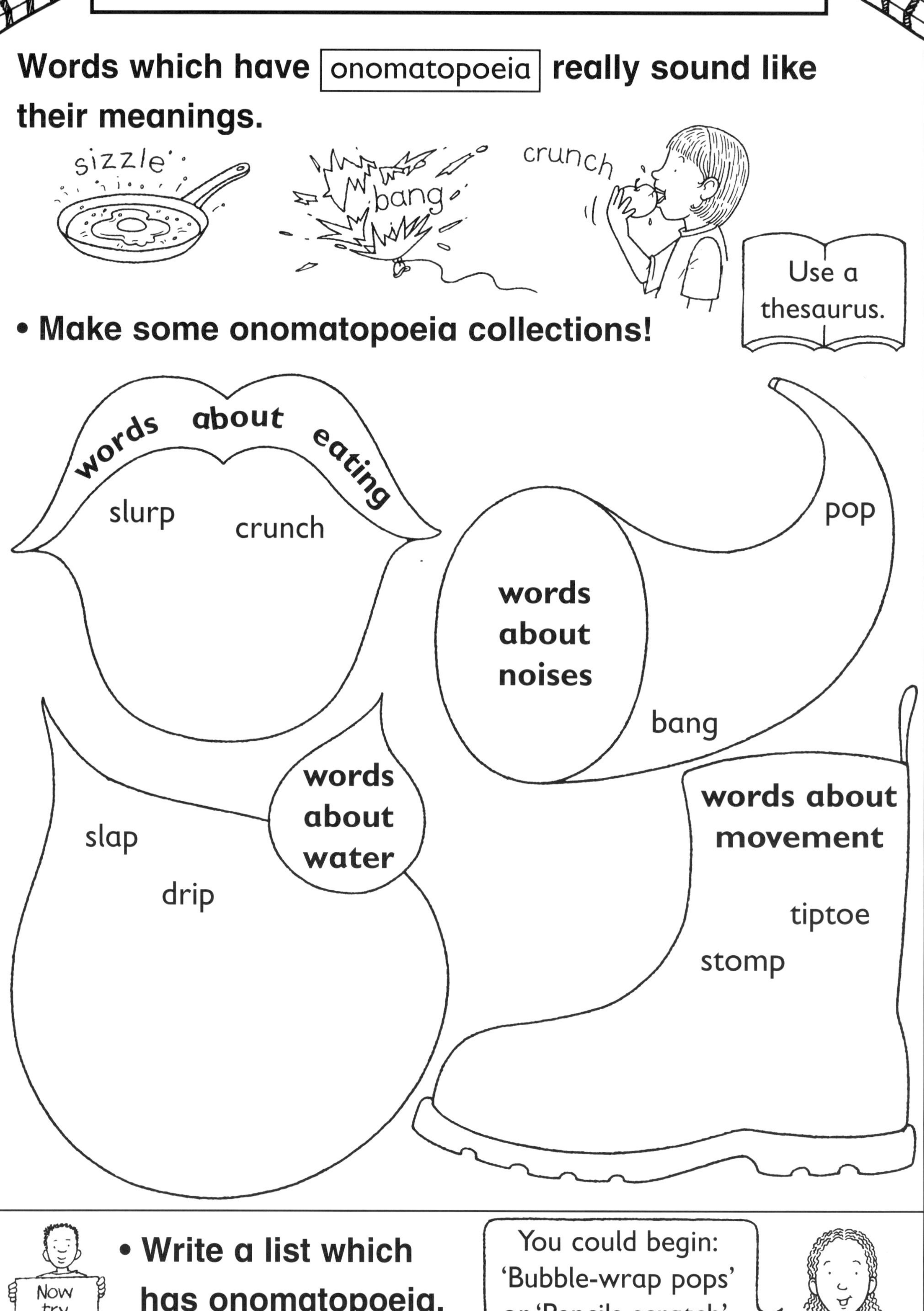

• **Make some onomatopoeia collections!**

• **Write a list which has onomatopoeia.**

You could begin: 'Bubble-wrap pops' or 'Pencils scratch'.

Teachers' note Read out a list of words with onomatopoeia and ask the children what they notice about the sounds of the words: for example, animal sounds such as moo, quack, roar and squeak. In the extension activity the children should write a list which is relevant to a particular place or topic: for example, the classroom, or an appliance such as a washing machine.

Developing Literacy
Poetry Year 3
© A & C Black

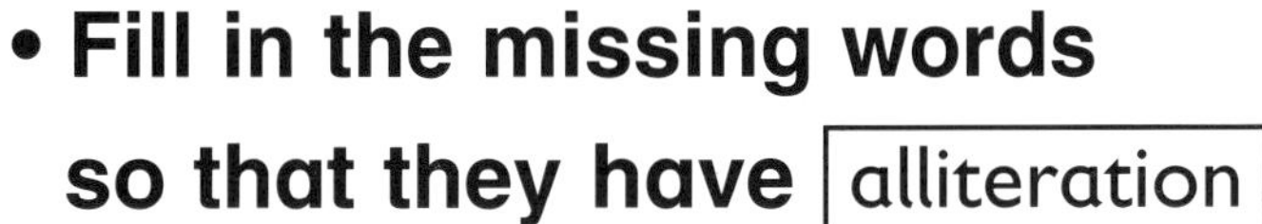

Alliterative allsorts

- **Fill in the missing words
  so that they have** alliteration .

Examples:

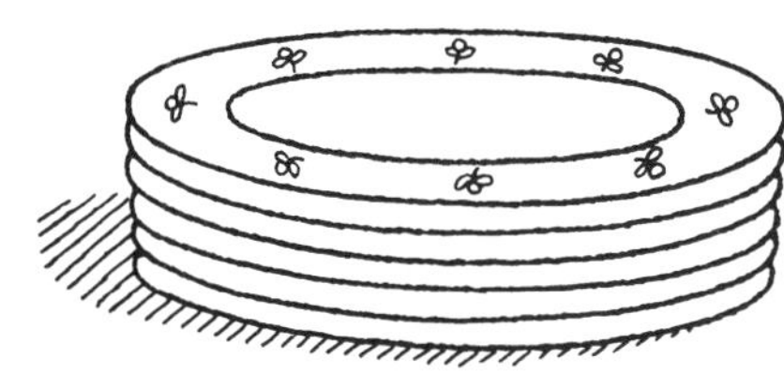

a (p)iece of (p)ie   a (j)ar of (j)am   a (p)ile of (p)lates

They must make sense.

Example: a vase of violets **but not** a vase of vests

a bunch of ________________   a mug of ________________

a bottle of ________________   a slice of ________________

a hunk of ________________   a bowl of ________________

a dish of ________________   a litre of ________________

a chunk of ________________   a pan of ________________

a cup of ________________   a plate of ________________

a lump of ________________   a tank of ________________

a basket of ________________   a can of ________________

- **List other containers or parts of things.**
- **Think of things to go with them. They must
  start with the same** sound .

Teachers' note Read a list of alliterative parts or containers and contents and ask the children
what they notice about the words: for example, a pile of paper, a heap of hay, a box of biscuits, a
spoonful of sugar and a portion of paella.

**Developing Literacy
Poetry Year 3
© A & C Black**

Still as a post and tall as a spire

Poets sometimes use comparisons **to describe things.**

• **Match the comparisons to the pictures.**

tall as a spire

necks like rods

snug as a nest

lonely as a cloud

broad as a barn door

teeth like splinters

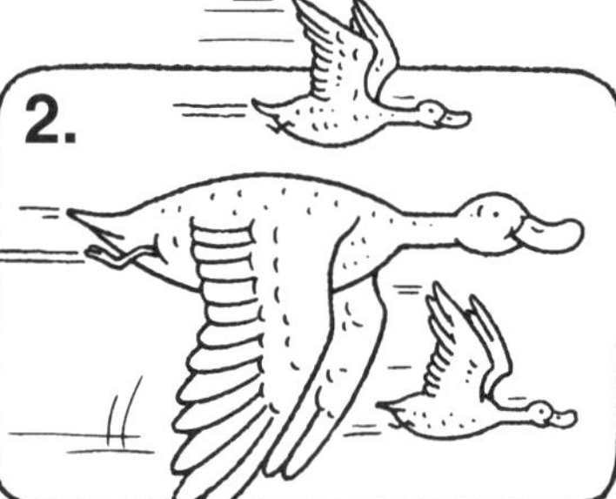

Picture	Comparison
1	lonely as a cloud

• **Write comparisons for these.**

...an old tree

...a flamingo standing still

...a strong gust of wind

...a cat rushing across a garden

...a scruffy child

...a noisy, clanking, old car.

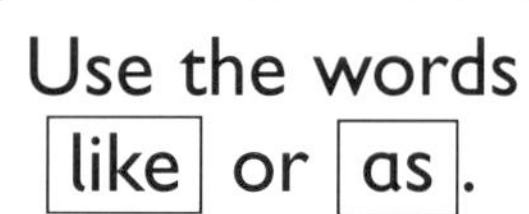

Teachers' note Revise similes and introduce comparisons which use 'like' rather than 'as'. The children could consider the different impressions created by comparisons: for example, 'whistled like a kettle', 'whistled like the wind', 'long fingers like snakes', 'long fingers like twigs'.

**Developing Literacy
Poetry Year 3
© A & C Black**

Comparisons

When say something is like something else, you are making a comparison.

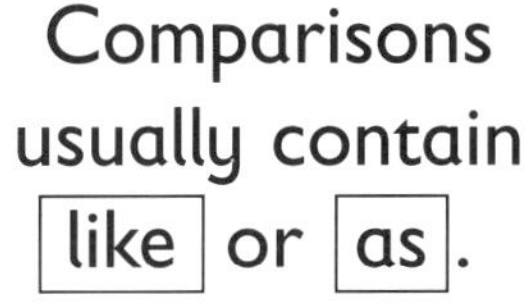

as dry as a bone

as light as a feather

• **Underline the comparisons in this poem.**

How to Make a Greyhound

It needs
A head like a snake, a neck like a drake,
A back like a beam, a belly like a bream,
A foot like a cat, and a tail like a rat.

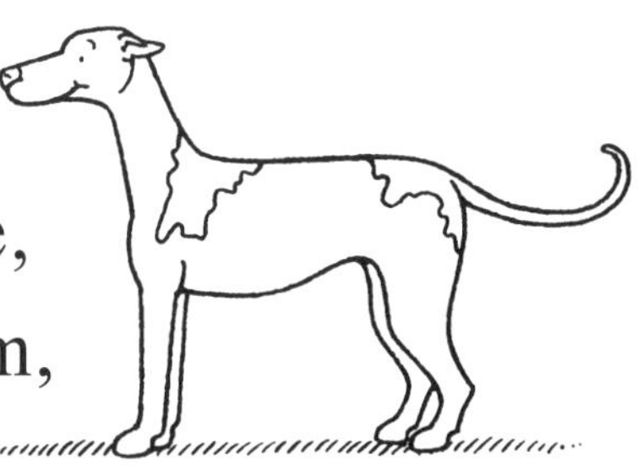

Anonymous

• **Complete this poem about a butterfly.**

It needs
Wings like ______________________________,
Feelers like ______________________________,
Eyes like ______________________________,
A body like a ______________________________,
And a sound like ______________________________.

• **Write another 'how to make an animal' poem.**

Ptarmigans and pterodactyls

- **Read the poem aloud.**

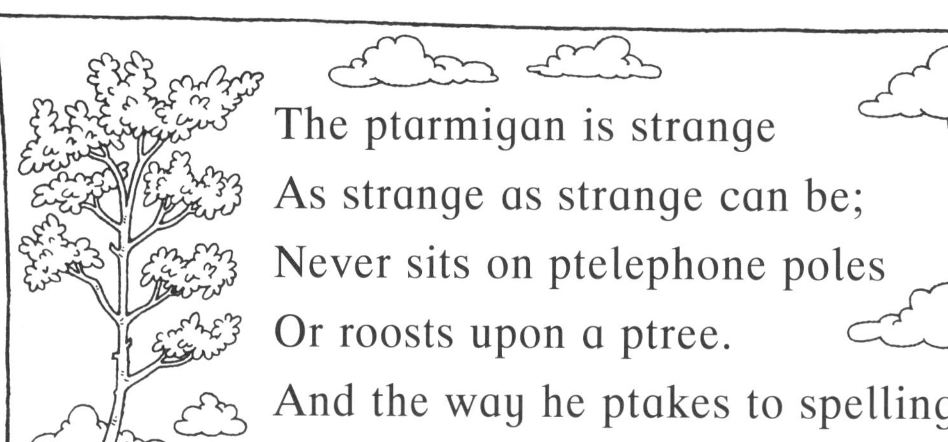

The ptarmigan is strange
As strange as strange can be;
Never sits on ptelephone poles
Or roosts upon a ptree.
And the way he ptakes to spelling
Is the strangest thing to me.

Anonymous

- **Change these to 'ptarmigan' words.**

tail ___ptail___   talk __________   tall __________

talons __________   tame __________   tap __________

tell __________   temper __________   ten __________

- **Make up six other 'ptarmigan' words.**

__________   __________   __________

__________   __________   __________

- **Make up a poem about a pterodactyl.**
Use the ptarmigan poem as a model.

Teachers' note Introduce the silent 'p' (for example, in 'psalm'). Revise silent letters such as the silent 'k' in 'knife' and the silent 'b' in 'bomb'. The children could use a dictionary to find words beginning with 't' to which they can add a silent initial 'p'. They could also play word games using silent 'p'.

**Developing Literacy
Poetry Year 3
© A & C Black**

Word jokes

- **Write the answers to these jokes.**

- **Write jokes about these.**

> a cracked pane and a packed crane

> a tie pin and a pie tin

> a long road and a wrong load

Teachers' note To introduce the activity write pairs of words on a large piece of paper. Cover the beginnings of the words with paper and invite the children to exchange the beginning of one word with that of another.

Developing Literacy
Poetry Year 3
© A & C Black

Absurd words

• **Complete the 'absurd word' captions.**

the sea bed

the hands of
a clock

the bonnet of
____

a car
____

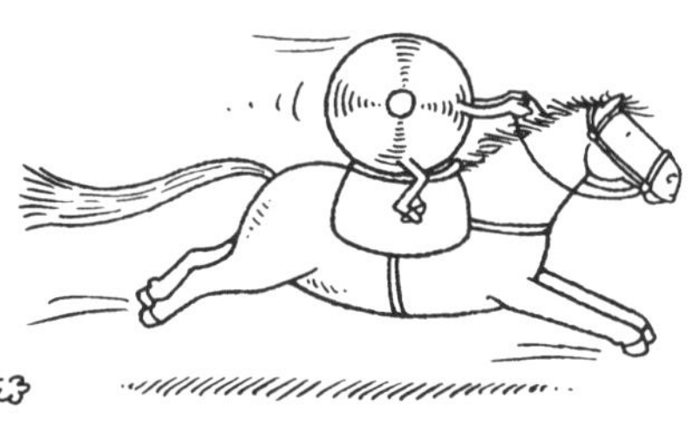

a disc
____

a daffodil
____

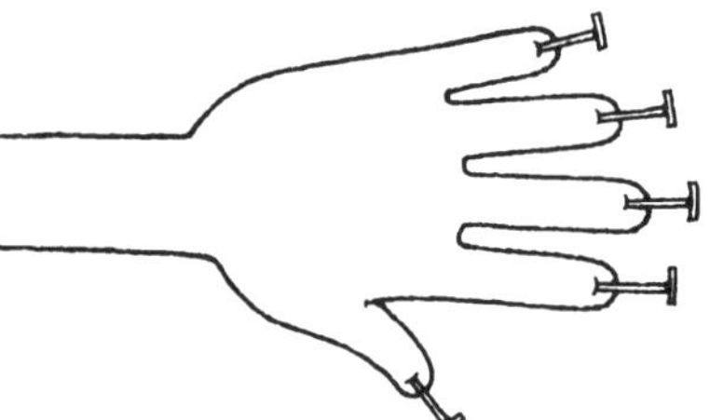

finger
____

the tongue of
____

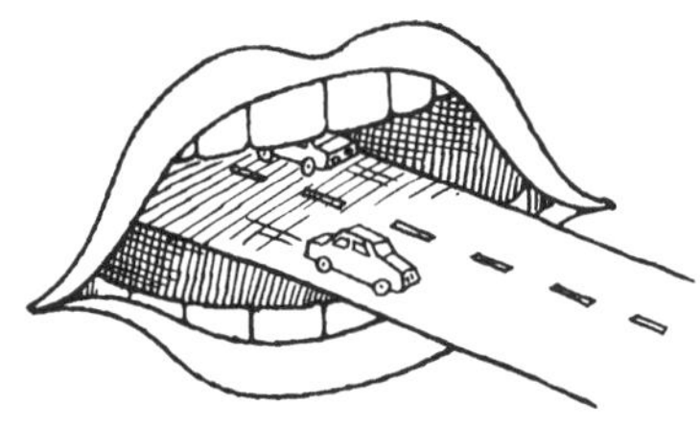

____
of a tunnel

____
of a building

____

• **Draw and write captions for**
four other 'absurd words'.

______________ finger

Teachers' note During the introductory session, discuss words the children know which have more than one meaning: for example, bridge, brow, crook, eye, foot, head, leaf. Ask the children to explain the first two examples, then model the third and fourth examples and ask them to explain those, too.

Developing Literacy
Poetry Year 3
© A & C Black

Legs riddle

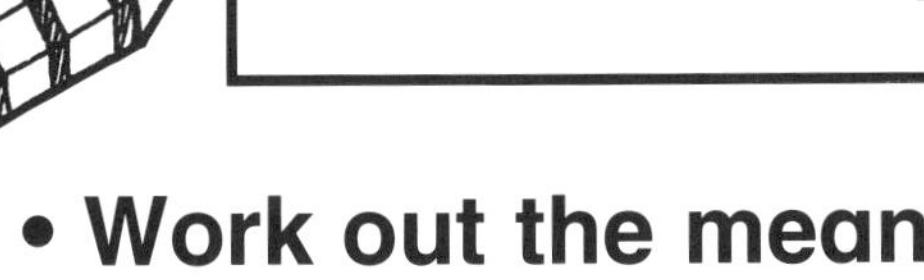

- **Work out the meaning of the riddle.**

  What are:

  two legs? _______________

  three legs? _______________

  four legs? _______________

  one leg? _______________

Two legs sat upon three legs
With one leg in a bag;
In comes four legs
And runs away with one leg;
Up jumps two legs,
Catches up three legs,
Throws it after four legs,
And makes him bring back
one leg.

Anonymous

- **Tell the story of the riddle.**

Lines 1 and 2

Lines 3 and 4

Lines 5 and 6

Lines 7 and 8

- **Write a 'wheels' riddle.**

Teachers' note Introduce the activity with short and simple riddles about items in the classroom:
for example, 'a sheaf of white leaves with black markings' (an exercise book), 'the more you use
it the shorter it becomes' (chalk or a pencil). In the extension activity the children could include a
wheelbarrow, a unicycle, a bicycle, a tricycle, a car, a bus, a truck and so on.

**Developing Literacy
Poetry Year 3
© A & C Black**

Twister

• **Read the tongue-twister aloud.**

Theophilus Thistledown, the successful thistle sifter,
In sifting a sieve of unsifted thistles,
Thrust three thousand unsifted thistles
Through the thick of his thumb.

Anonymous

Which two phonemes **twist the tongue in the poem?**

• **Make two lists of words which contain these two phonemes.**

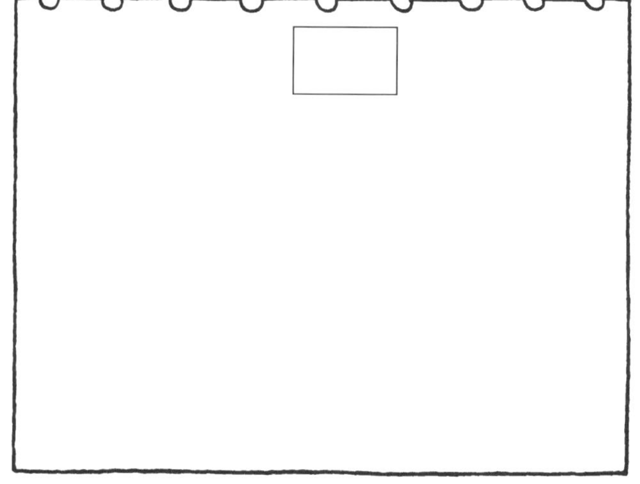

• **Make up a tongue-twister using some of the words you have listed.**

____

____

____

____

Teachers' note Read the tongue-twister and ask the children to have a try. Ask them which two phonemes are repeated. They could think of other pairs of phonemes which make words difficult to read quickly: for example 'w' and 'r' and 'gr' and 'g'.

**Developing Literacy
Poetry Year 3
© A & C Black**

A parrot's advice

Mother Parrot's Advice to her Children

Never get up till the sun gets up,

Or the mists will give you a cold,

And a parrot whose lungs have once been touched

Will never live to be old.

Never eat plums that are not quite ripe,

For perhaps they will give you a pain;

And never dispute what the hornbill says,

Or you'll never dispute again.

Never despise the power of speech;

Learn every word as it comes,

For this is the pride of the parrot race,

That it speaks in a thousand tongues.

Never stay up when the sun goes down,

But sleep in your own bed,

And if you've been good, as a parrot should,

You will dream that your tail is red.

A K Nyabongo

**Developing Literacy
Poetry Year 3**
© A & C Black

A parent's advice

- **Write a poem of advice from a mother or father to its child.**

> Make notes first.
> Your poem need
> not rhyme.

Title: _______________________ Advice to _______________________

Never _______________________

Or _______________________

And a _______________________

Will _______________________

Never _______________________

For _______________________

And never _______________________

Or _______________________

Never _______________________

____

For this is the pride of the _______________________ family,

That it _______________________

Never _______________________

But _______________________

And if you've been good, as a _______________________ should,

You will dream that _______________________

Teachers' note The children should first have read and discussed the poem on page 39 and have a copy of it to refer to. Discuss things which might be good or bad for the children to do, what might happen if they ignore advice and how they might be rewarded if they are good.

**Developing Literacy
Poetry Year 3
© A & C Black**

40

1.

Cats

Cats sleep
Anywhere,
Any table,
Any chair,
Top of piano,
Window-ledge,
In the middle,
On the edge,
Open drawer,
Empty shoe,
Anybody's
Lap will do,
Fitted in a
Cardboard box,
In the cupboard
With your frocks –
Anywhere!
They don't care!
Cats sleep
Anywhere.

Eleanor Farjeon

2.

At midnight in the alley
   A Tom-cat comes to wail,
And he chants the hate of a million years
   As he swings his snaky tail...

He will lie on a rug tomorrow
   And lick his silky fur,
And veil the brute in his yellow eyes
   And play he's tame, and purr.

But at midnight in the alley
   He will crouch again and wail,
And beat the time for his demon's song
   With a swing of his demon's tail.

From *The Tom-Cat* by Don Marquis

The same but different: 2

What do the two poems tell you?

- **Complete the chart.**

	✔ or x		Words or phrases which tell me this	
	1	2	Poem 1	Poem 2
The poet has watched cats sleeping.				
The poet has watched a cat outdoors.				
Cats do not take much notice of people.				
Cats pretend to like people.				
Cats are evil.				
Cats are awake at night.				
Cats sleep a lot.				
Cats do not need a special place to sleep in.				
Cats have soft fur.				

- **Is either poem a good advert for cats? Why?**

Teachers' note Use this with page 41. It provides a framework on which the children can organise their views and helps them to explain the different views the two poets have of the same subject.

**Developing Literacy
Poetry Year 3
© A & C Black**

Wind words: 1

- **Cut out the two pictures.**
- **Cut out the word cards.**
- **With a partner, match the words to the pictures.**
- **Write ten other word cards for each picture.**

Use a thesaurus.

Teachers' note This should be used with page 44. During the introductory session encourage the children to suggest words which describe what is happening in each picture and which convey the atmosphere of the scenes.

Developing Literacy Poetry Year 3 © A & C Black

Wind words: 2

blustery	roar	flutter
whisper	swish	puff
wail	fling	rage
howl	moan	breathe
tickle	lift	dance
breeze	gale	rush
gentle	blow	crush
twitch	grab	shout

Teachers' note The children should say the words aloud as they discuss with their partner which ones belong with which picture. Encourage them to think about the sounds of the words and the effects they create. They could use these words (and any new ones they have added) as the basis for a poem about the wind after observing it.

**Developing Literacy
Poetry Year 3
© A & C Black**

Splash poem

- **Write all the words you can think of about rain.**

slop
puddle
shiny

- **Use some of the words to write a poem about rain. Write a word or phrase on each splash and puddle.**

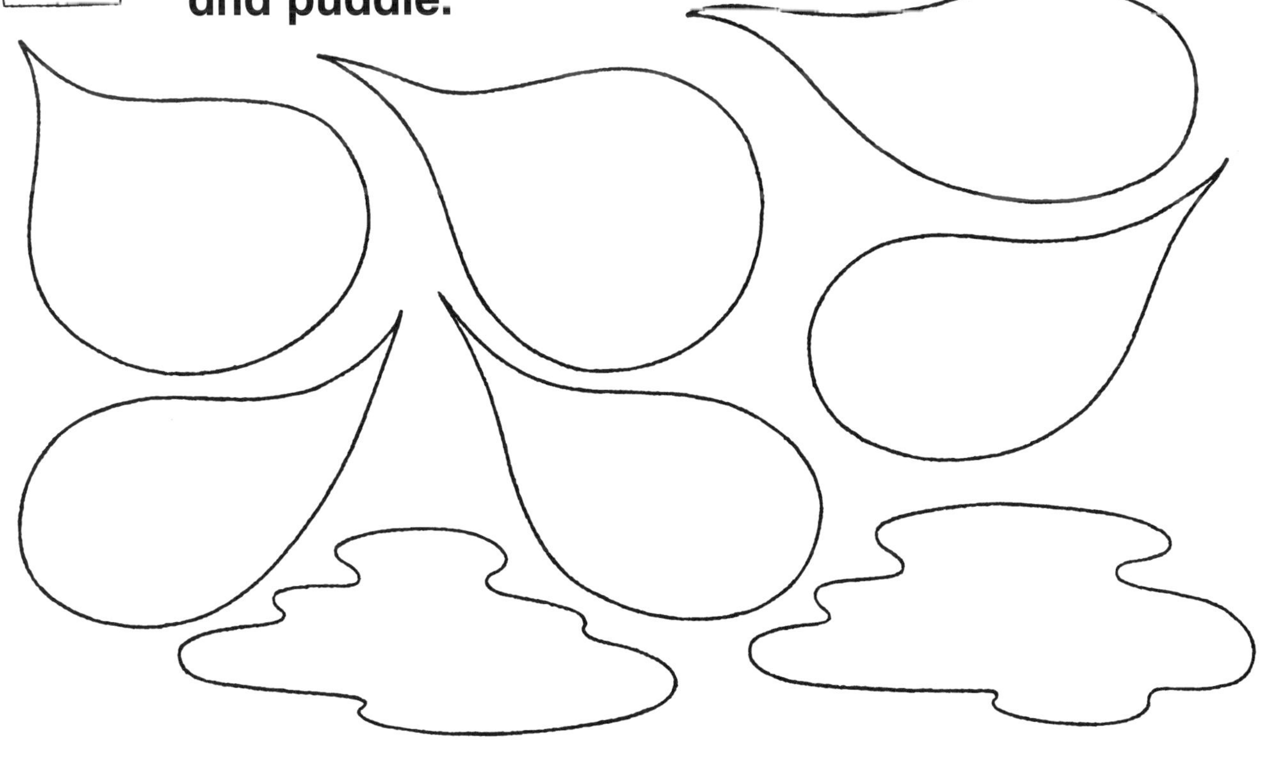

Teachers' note Introduce the activity by reading shape poems with the children (see **Introduction** page 8). During the introductory session provide a bowl of water and invite the children to splash the water around. Ask them to suggest words to describe what they see, hear and feel.

**Developing Literacy
Poetry Year 3
© A & C Black**

45

Shape sentences

• **Complete the shape sentences.**

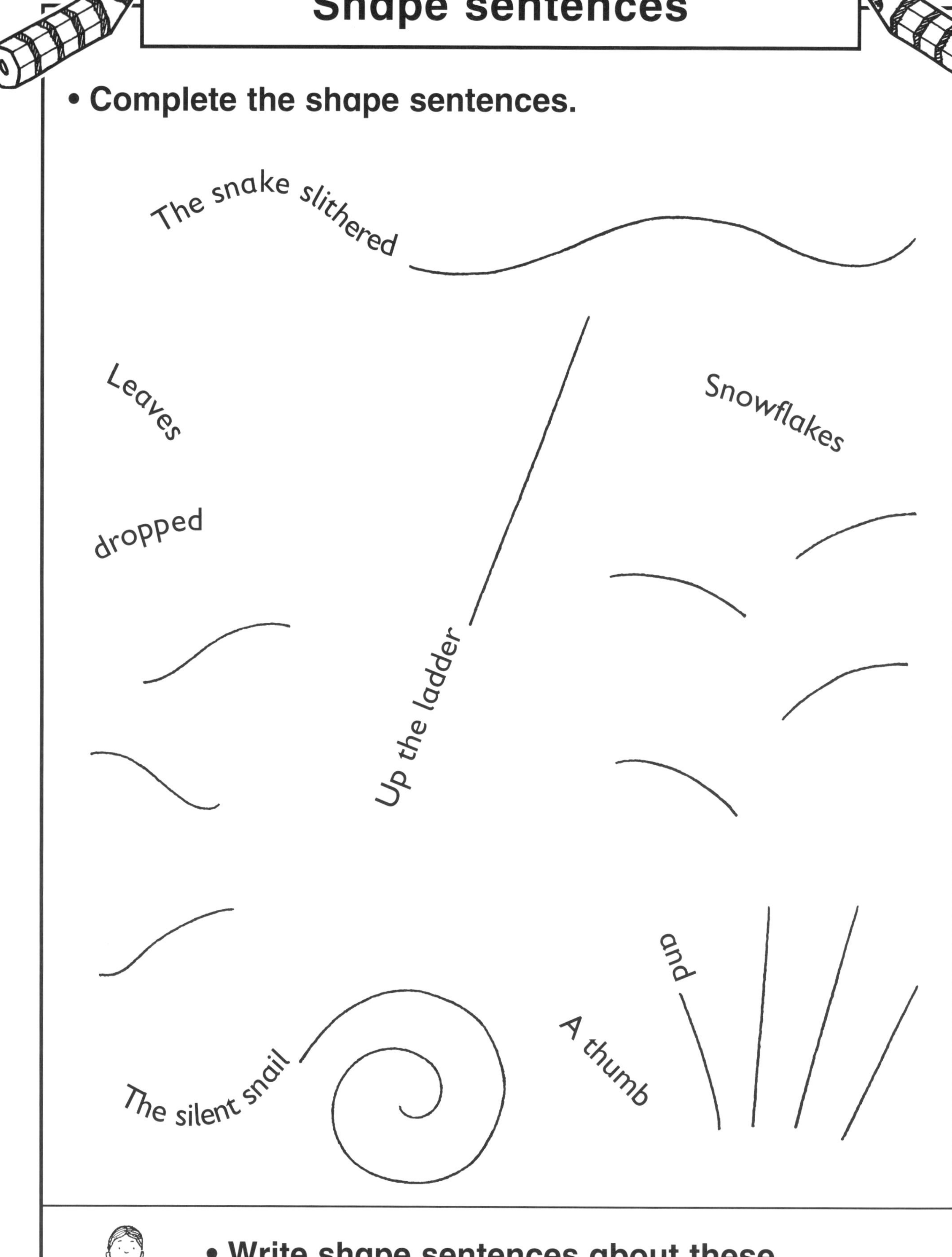

• **Write shape sentences about these.**

a fish   a spider   a star

Teachers' note Introduce the activity by inviting the children to suggest ways in which to complete the first sentence. Record their responses and discuss ways in which they can be refined and improved before choosing the most effective. Encourage the children to approach the other examples in the same way.

Developing Literacy
Poetry Year 3
© A & C Black

Word shapes

• **Write the words which are hidden in the shapes.**

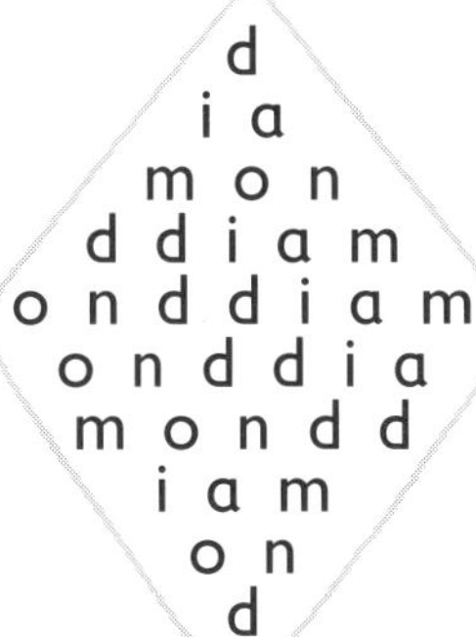

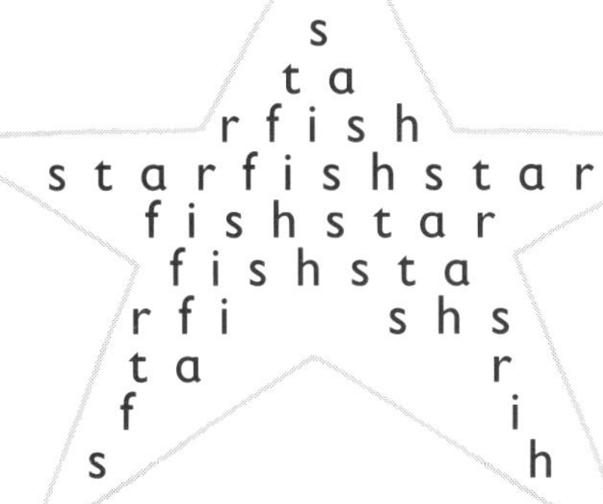

____________________   ____________________   ____________________

____________________   ____________________

____

• **Write word shapes for these.**

| a pair of jeans | a blue balloon |

Teachers' note The children could make their own word shapes by drawing an outline using a
heavy line, and placing it underneath the paper on which they are going to write the words.

Developing Literacy
Poetry Year 3
© A & C Black

Calligrams

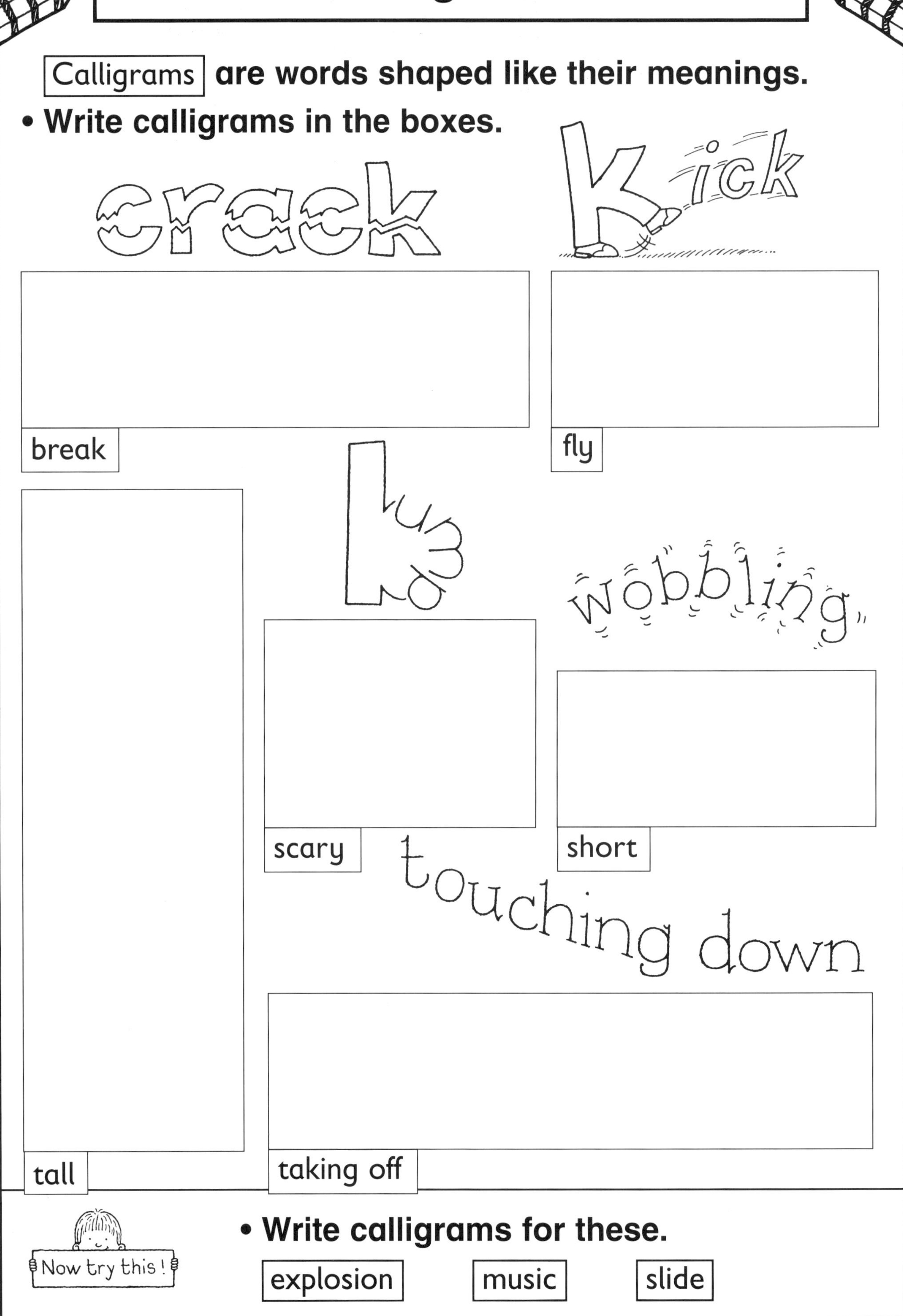

Calligrams are words shaped like their meanings.

• **Write calligrams in the boxes.**

• **Write calligrams for these.**

explosion   music   slide

Now try this!

Teachers' note Before the lesson, collect and display examples of calligrams from advertisements and enlarge and display calligrams from poetry books. Encourage the children to try out on scrap paper the different ways in which they could write the nouns and verbs they find in a dictionary or thesaurus.

Developing Literacy
Poetry Year 3
© A & C Black